AF269865

WNBA Hot Ticket

ATLANTA DREAM

JOSH ANDERSON

Lerner Publications ◆ Minneapolis

To Leo and Dane, the biggest superstars I've ever met.

The stats and information in this book are accurate through July 2024.

Lerner Publications Company
An imprint of Lerner Publishing Group, Inc.
241 First Avenue North
Minneapolis, MN 55401 USA

For reading levels and more information, look up this title at www.lernerbooks.com.

Main body text set in Aptifer Slab LT Pro / Typeface provided by Linotype AG

Library of Congress Cataloging-in-Publication Data

Names: Anderson, Josh, author.
Title: Atlanta Dream / Josh Anderson.
Description: Minneapolis, MN : Lerner Publications, [2025] | Series: WNBA hot ticket (Lerner sports) | Includes bibliographical references and index. | Audience: Ages 7–11 | Audience: Grades 2–3 | Summary: "The story of the Atlanta Dream can be told with buzzer-beating shots, gleeful fans, and successful seasons. But the team has never won the WNBA Championship. Meet the players who hope to change that soon"—Provided by publisher.
Identifiers: LCCN 2024030340 (print) | LCCN 2024030341 (ebook) | ISBN 9798765669754 (library binding) | ISBN 9798765669761 (paperback) | ISBN 9798765669785 (epub)
Subjects: LCSH: Atlanta Dream (Basketball team)—Juvenile literature. | Women's National Basketball Association—Juvenile literature. | Women basketball players—United States—Juvenile literature.
Classification: LCC GV885.52.A65 A53 2025 (print) | LCC GV885.52.A65 (ebook) | DDC 796.323/6409758231—dc23/eng/2024070

TABLE OF CONTENTS

A RETURN TO THE FINALS

The Atlanta Dream's trips to the 2010 and 2011 WNBA Finals ended in losses. To get back to the Finals in 2013, the Dream would need to beat the defending WNBA champion Indiana Fever in the Eastern Conference Finals.

Game 1 was a battle. The two teams knew each other well. They were facing off in the conference playoffs for the third straight season. While the Dream held a lead through the fourth quarter of Game 1, the Fever wouldn't back down. With under 90 seconds to go, Fever guard Shavonte Zellous hit a long shot to cut the Dream's lead to 78–75. Losing Game 1 at home would make winning the best-of-three series very difficult for the Dream.

Angel McCoughtry, the Dream's leading scorer, turned to her left and dribbled toward the hoop. She was closely guarded by the Fever's Karima Christmas. McCoughtry jumped and bounced the ball off the backboard and through the net. The ref blew their whistle to signal a foul by Christmas. McCoughtry sank her free throw, putting the Dream up 81–75. The Dream won the game 84–79. They won the series after a victory in Game 2 before losing to the Minnesota Lynx in the WNBA Finals.

While the Dream are still looking for their first WNBA title, they have played in the Finals three times. The 2023 season marked the team's first playoff appearance in five years. Head coach Tanisha Wright and Dream fans are hoping a return to the Finals may be close for Atlanta.

Angel McCoughtry (*right*) guards Indiana's Briann January during the 2013 WNBA playoffs.

Atlanta guard Armintie Herrington reaches up for the ball. Herrington averaged 2.3 assists and 1.9 steals per game during the 2013 playoffs.

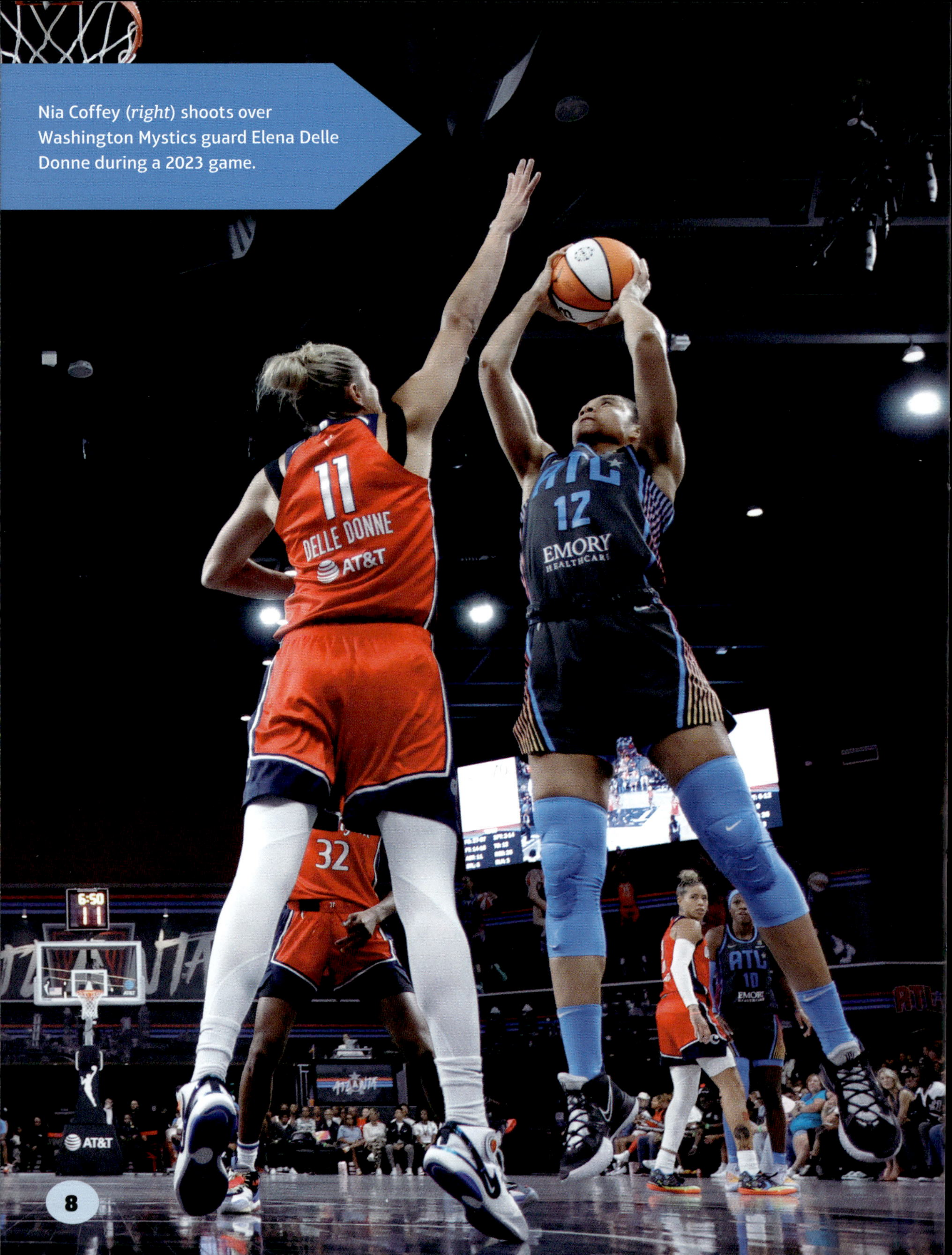

Nia Coffey (*right*) shoots over Washington Mystics guard Elena Delle Donne during a 2023 game.

8

CHAPTER 1

HOOP DREAMS IN ATLANTA

The WNBA had 14 teams during the 2006 season before the Charlotte Sting stopped play, leaving the league with only 13 teams. In October 2007, the WNBA announced that a new team would start in Atlanta, Georgia. Atlanta became the league's 14th team and began playing in 2008.

The team held an online contest to decide on a name. The name Dream was chosen by fans to honor the famous "I Have a Dream" speech by Atlanta native Dr. Martin Luther King Jr. The Dream play their home games at Gateway Center Arena in College Park, Georgia. The building holds 3,500 fans for basketball.

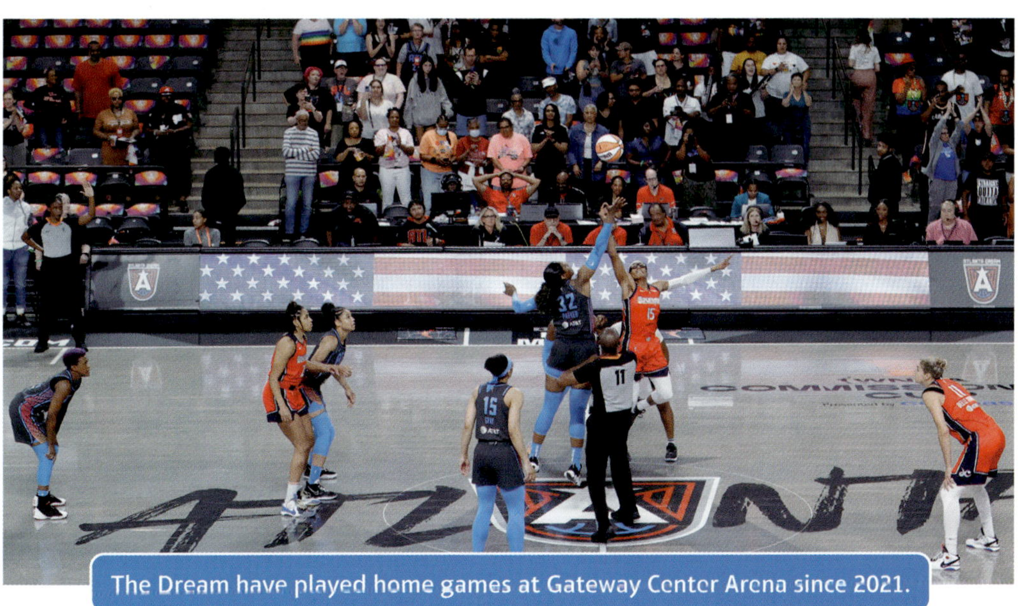

The Dream have played home games at Gateway Center Arena since 2021.

Atlanta's first season in 2008 was more of a nightmare than a dream. It's normal for expansion teams to struggle at first. The Dream lost their first 17 games, setting a WNBA record at the time for most losses in a row.

After finishing with a 4–30 record in 2008, the team added a group of talented players ahead of the 2009 season. They included women's basketball legend Chamique Holdsclaw and defensive star Sancho Lyttle. The Dream also picked Angel McCoughtry in the WNBA Draft. She would become one of the team's best players for the next decade.

Chamique Holdsclaw averaged 13.9 points and 4.4 rebounds per game during her season with the Dream.

Angel McCoughtry led the WNBA in steals and points per game twice during her 10 seasons in Atlanta.

Many of these players led the way for Atlanta's first playoff appearance in 2009. The team reached the WNBA Finals in 2010, 2011, and 2013. Since 2013, the Dream have appeared in the playoffs four times but have only won one series.

During her time at the University of Kentucky, Rhyne Howard (*left*) was the conference freshman of the year in 2019 and the conference player of the year in 2020 and 2021.

In need of strong players to build around, the Dream made some big moves. Forward Cheyenne Parker joined the team in 2021. Then the Dream traded for the first pick in the 2022 WNBA Draft and chose University of Kentucky star Rhyne Howard. In 2023, Atlanta traded two first-round draft picks for guard Allisha Gray. All three have rewarded the team by becoming All-Star players for Atlanta.

The team's 2023 playoff appearance ended in a first-round loss to the Dallas Wings. But there's enough talent on the roster for the Dream to play well over the next few seasons and build on to the team's track record of success.

PARTNERING FOR CHANGE

The Dream have partnered with health-care company Anthem, Inc., to try to impact people's health in Atlanta and the surrounding areas. They are working to make sure people in need have enough to eat. The Dream and Anthem also want to help improve mental health and women's health in the area.

The team took part in food drives at six of the Dream's 2023 games. Money raised from the drives helped stock shelves at a food pantry in College Park that assists families who might need food. Dream players also helped at a local school for National Read Across America Day. They read to the students and encouraged them to read on their own.

The Dream's programs to support women's health include Yoga on the Court and other events that encourage young women to take care of their minds and bodies.

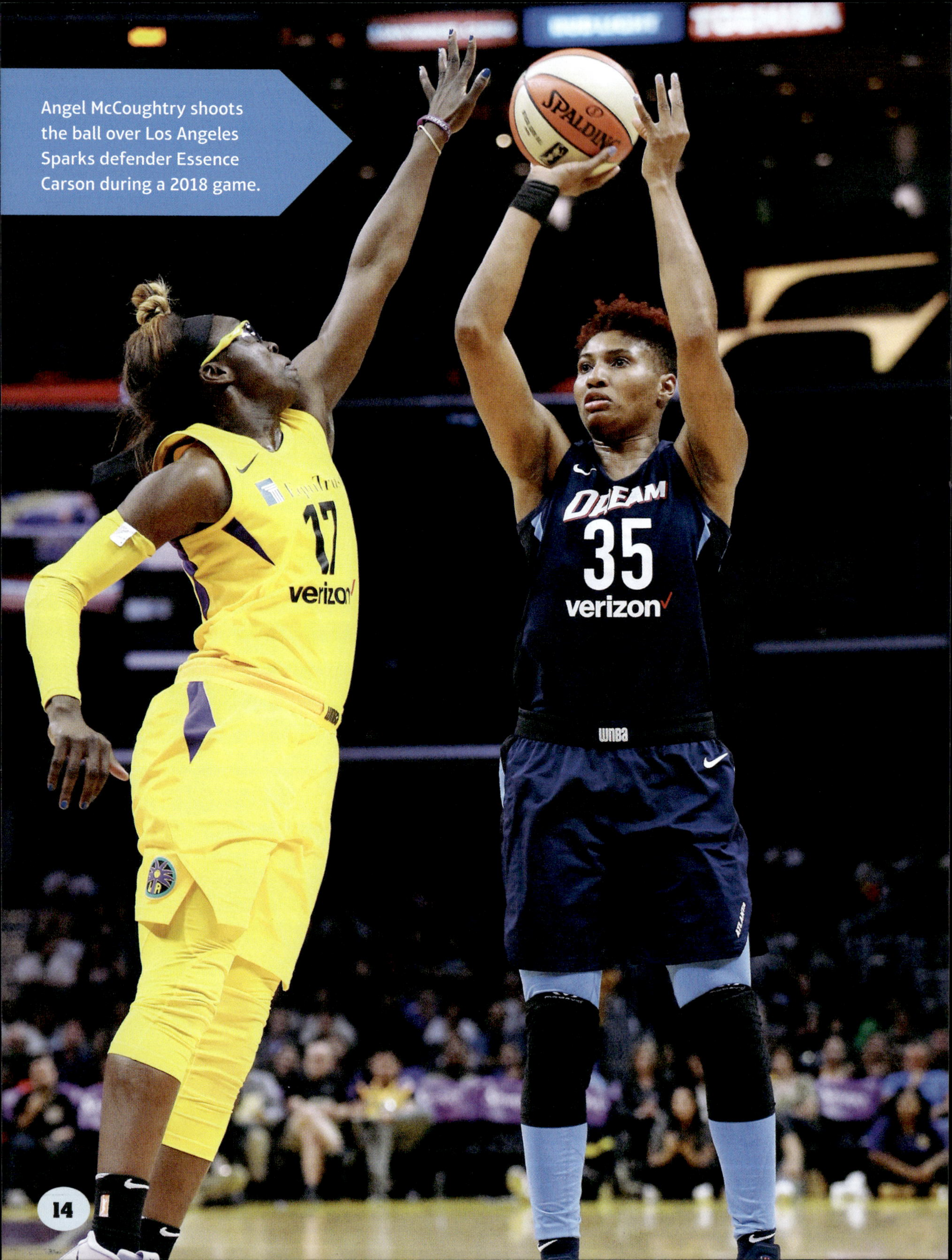

Angel McCoughtry shoots
the ball over Los Angeles
Sparks defender Essence
Carson during a 2018 game.

CHAPTER 2

INCREDIBLE PLAYERS

No player in Dream history has done more on the court than Angel McCoughtry. At the University of Louisville, she became the school's all-time leading scorer. Then the Dream chose McCoughtry first overall in the 2009 WNBA Draft. McCoughtry was the league's Rookie of the Year in 2009.

As the team's leading scorer, McCoughtry led the Dream to the WNBA Finals in 2010, 2011, and 2013. McCoughtry was the WNBA's scoring leader twice and steals leader three times. She was picked for five All-Star Games and seven All-Defensive teams. McCoughtry also led the US women's team to gold medals at the 2012 and 2016 Olympic Games.

Angel McCoughtry (*second from left*) and Erika de Souza (*center*) walk onto the court with their teammates during the 2011 WNBA Finals.

One of McCoughtry's Atlanta teammates was Erika de Souza, who played for the Dream from 2008 to 2015. The Brazilian center was a top shot blocker and rebounder during her time with the Dream. Her 368 career blocks rank 18th in WNBA history. She was chosen for three All-Star Games during her time with the Dream.

Tiffany Hayes joined the Dream in 2012 and played in Atlanta for 10 seasons. Although she was only an All-Star once, Hayes averaged 13.3 points per game during her career. She is the Dream's all-time leader in three-pointers with 325. Hayes was also great at drawing fouls. She finished in the top 10 in the WNBA in free throws four times.

Tiffany Hayes dribbles around Las Vegas Aces defender Riquna Williams in 2022. Hayes scored 3,828 points during her 10 seasons in Atlanta.

The Dream's first head coach holds the team record for wins. Marynell Meadors led the Dream to 73 wins in her five years with the team. She also helped the Dream reach the Finals twice. She coached Atlanta from 2008 until 2012.

In 2024, the Dream had several exciting players on the roster. Cheyenne Parker came to the Dream in 2021 after playing her first six seasons with the Chicago Sky. Parker is one of the best rebounders and shot blockers in the WNBA. The forward was chosen for her first All-Star Game in 2023.

Exciting young guard Rhyne Howard became the first overall pick in the WNBA Draft when Atlanta chose her in 2022. As a rookie, she finished third in the WNBA in three-pointers, seventh in steals, and tenth in points. She was picked as the league's Rookie of the Year. Howard was also an All-Star during her first two seasons in the league in 2022 and 2023.

Atlanta traded two draft picks for Allisha Gray in 2023. Gray's first season in Atlanta was the best of her career. Her 17.1 points and 3.1 assists per game were both career highs. Gray was chosen for her first All-Star Game that year.

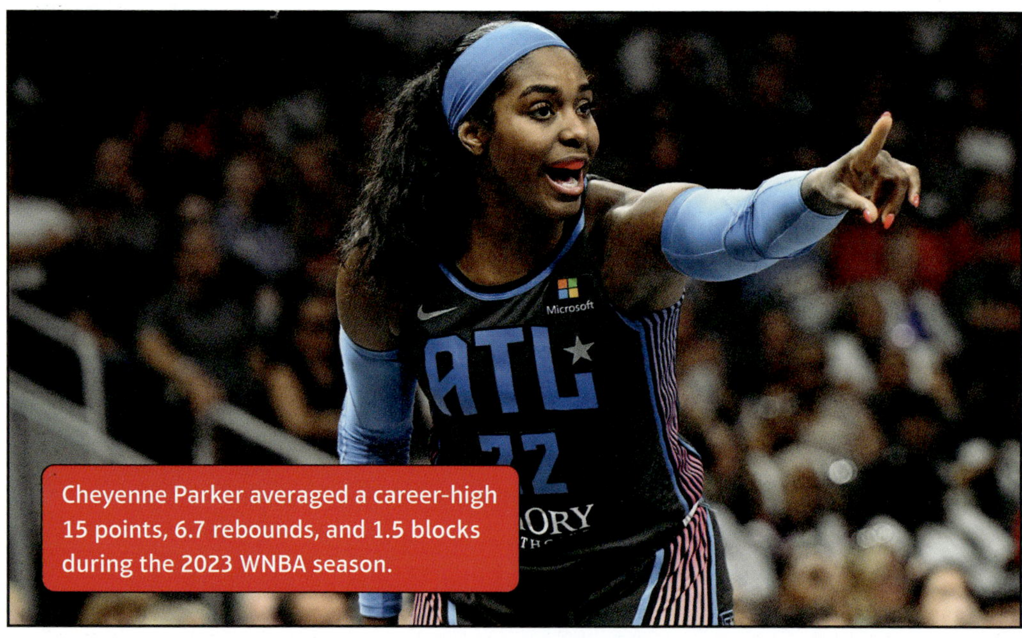

Cheyenne Parker averaged a career-high 15 points, 6.7 rebounds, and 1.5 blocks during the 2023 WNBA season.

Shoni Schimmel averaged 8.3 points per game in 2014.

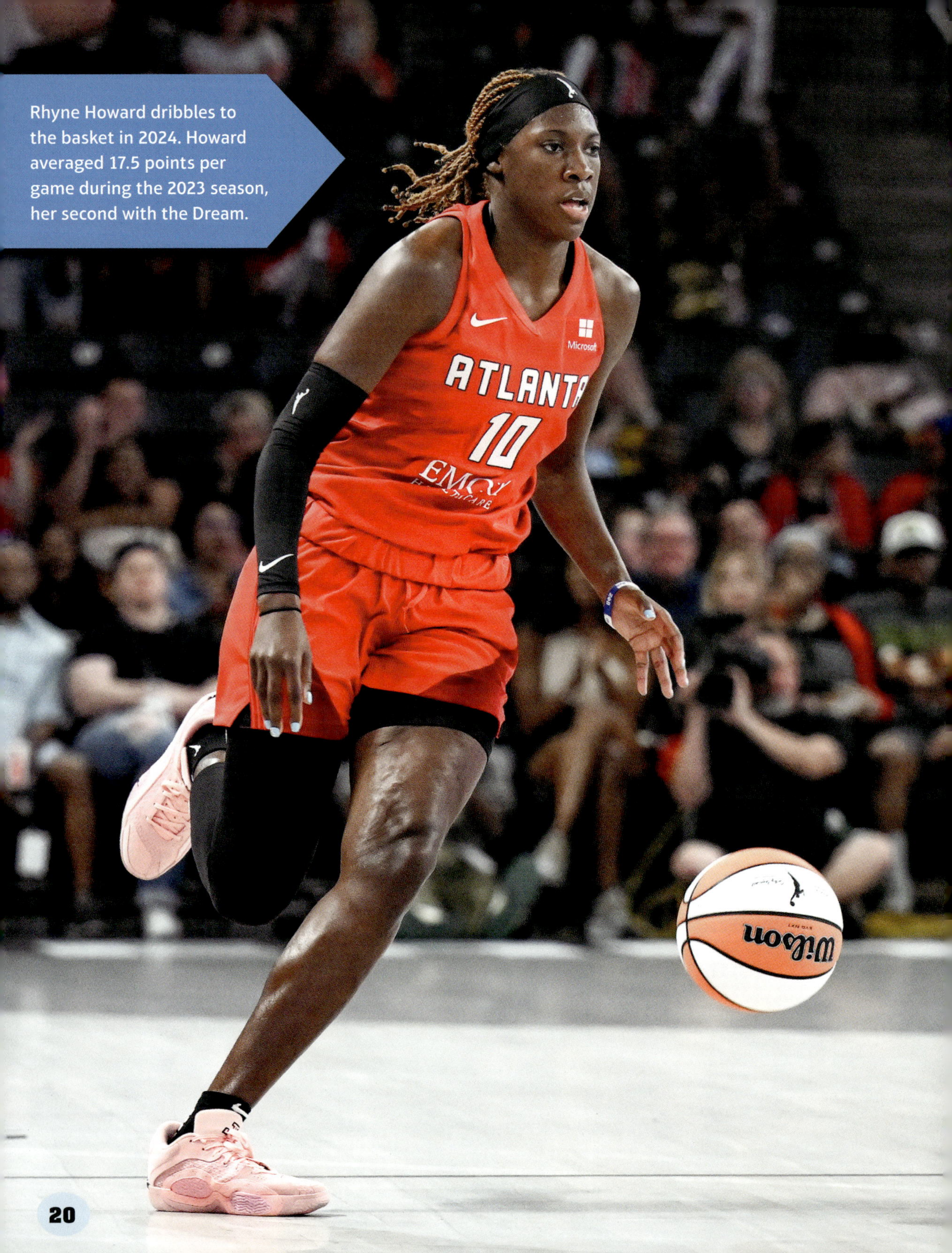

Rhyne Howard dribbles to the basket in 2024. Howard averaged 17.5 points per game during the 2023 season, her second with the Dream.

CHAPTER 3

AMAZING MOMENTS

It's rare when a player's performance is so incredible that it overshadows the result of the game. But that's exactly what happened in the 2023 WNBA playoffs. The Dream's 19 wins that year were its most since 2018. Atlanta fans had high hopes for the team's first-round series against the Dallas Wings. But the Dream were not considered strong contenders to win the WNBA title against great teams such as the Las Vegas Aces and the New York Liberty.

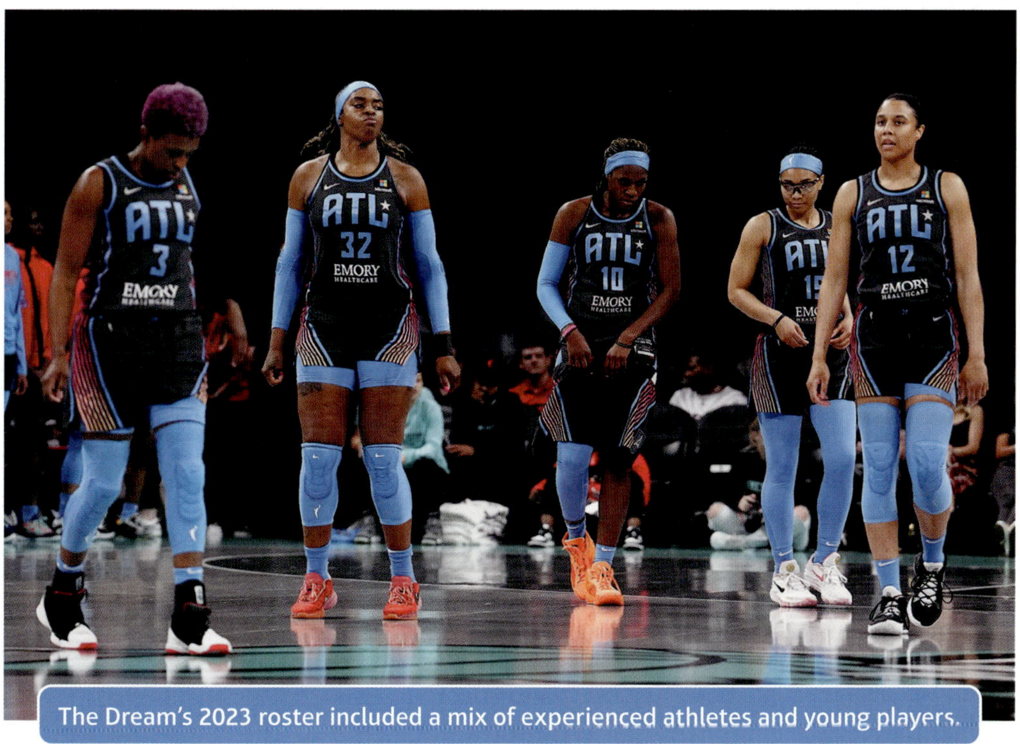

The Dream's 2023 roster included a mix of experienced athletes and young players.

In Game 1 against Dallas, the Dream built an early lead and held it throughout most of the first half. Dallas tied the game going into halftime. The teams traded leads throughout the third and fourth quarters before Dallas pulled away in the game's final minutes.

Although the Dream lost the game, young star Rhyne Howard made history. She scored 19 points in the opening quarter. Howard tied former Dream player Angel McCoughtry for the most points scored in a first quarter in playoff history.

In the final minute of the third quarter, Howard got a pass behind the three-point line with the game tied 67–67. She started to drive to her defender's right, causing the defender to move toward the hoop. Suddenly, Howard pulled back, leaving a huge space between her and her defender. Howard rose up from behind the three-point line and sank a basket for three points.

HOOPS SCOOP
Angel McCoughtry's 89 steals in 2013 were the sixth most in a WNBA season.
Rhyne Howard averaged 28.5 points per game during the 2023 WNBA playoffs.

Howard finished the game with 36 points. She became the youngest player in league history to score 30 or more points in a playoff game. She also scored the most points all-time for a player in her first WNBA playoff game. While the record-setting performance wasn't enough to win the game, it was a bright spot for fans craving success for their team.

The highest-scoring game for a player in Dream history also came during a loss. In the middle of the Dream's first season, when the team finished 4–30, leading scorer Betty Lennox had the best night of her career. Playing in a 109–101 overtime loss to the Connecticut Sun, Lennox scored 44 points. She made 17 of her 32 shot attempts and hit five three-pointers. She also finished with nine rebounds, seven assists, and three steals. Only nine players in league history have scored more points in a single game.

Although they lost in the first round, their 2023 playoff appearance gave the Dream hope for the 2024 season.

Head coach Tanisha Wright (*left*) instructs Cheyenne Parker during a 2022 game against the Las Vegas Aces.

CHAPTER 4

DREAMING OF THE FUTURE

Few teams in pro sports have been as successful in their first six seasons as the Atlanta Dream were from 2008 to 2013. With five trips to the playoffs and three to the WNBA Finals, it was a dream start for the team. But in the decade to follow, the Dream only managed two winning seasons and one playoff series victory. Fans in Atlanta are ready to cheer on a winner.

After the Dream only won eight games in 2021, new head coach Tanisha Wright helped the team improve to 14 wins in 2022. That year, she won the Associated Press Coach of the Year award. She helped the Dream get back to the playoffs in 2023 for the first time in five years.

Tanisha Wright (*right*) played for three WNBA teams from 2005 until 2014. She served as an assistant coach for the Las Vegas Aces before she became head coach of the Dream.

Wright has enough talent on the roster to build on the successes of her first two seasons. Rhyne Howard and Allisha Gray are true stars. Cheyenne Parker adds leadership and scoring. The team also added future Hall of Fame center Tina Charles in 2024. The former league MVP will help as a scorer and rebounder. While the team may be one star player away from winning a WNBA title, there's nothing stopping the Dream from being a playoff team for many years to come.

The Dream won five of their first 10 games during the 2024 season, including an 11-point victory over the Los Angeles Sparks in their season opener.

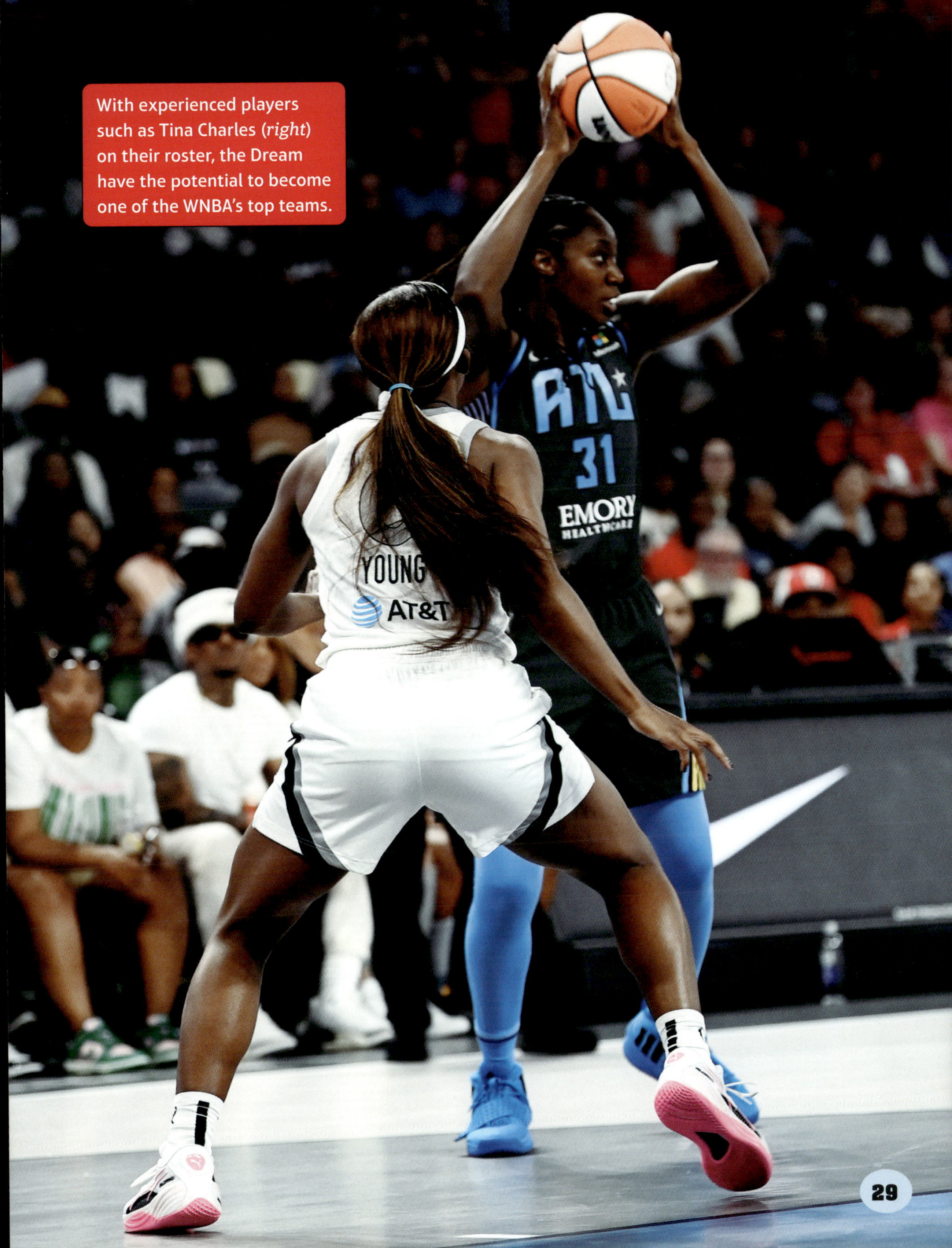

With experienced players such as Tina Charles (*right*) on their roster, the Dream have the potential to become one of the WNBA's top teams.

GLOSSARY

All-Star: a player chosen as one of the best in the league to compete in a game against other top players

assist: a pass that leads directly to a basket

draft: when teams take turns choosing new players

expansion team: a team added to an existing sports league

forward: a player who usually plays near the basket

free throw: an open shot taken from behind a set line after a foul by an opponent

playoffs: games held after the season to determine each year's champion

rebounder: a player who grabs and controls the ball after a missed shot

rookie: a first-year player

roster: a list of players on a team

title: championship

LEARN MORE

Atlanta Dream
https://dream.wnba.com/

Doeden, Matt. *Basketball's Biggest Rivalries*. North Mankato, MN: Capstone Press, 2024.

Scheff, Matt. *NBA and WNBA Finals: Basketball's Biggest Playoffs*. Minneapolis: Lerner Publications, 2021

Whiting, Jim. *The Story of the Atlanta Dream*. Mankato, MN: Creative Education and Creative Paperbacks, 2024.

WNBA
https://www.wnba.com/

Women's National Basketball Association Facts for Kids
https://kids.kiddle.co/Women%27s_National_Basketball
_Association

INDEX

PHOTO ACKNOWLEDGMENTS

Image credits: Darrell Walker/Icon Sportswire/Getty Images, p.4; TMB/Icon SMI DBF/Newscom, p.6; TMB/Icon SMI DBF/Newscom, p.7; Alex Slitz/Getty Images Sport/Getty Images, p.8; Alex Slitz/Getty Images Sport/Getty Images, p. 9; Darrell Walker/Icon Sportswire/Getty Images, p.10; Darrell Walker/Icon Sportswire/Getty Images, p.11; Alex Slitz/Getty Images Sport/Getty Images, p.12; John McClellan/Flickr, p.13; Leon Bennett./Getty Images Sport/Getty Images, p.14; Hannah Foslien/Getty Images Sport/Getty Images, p.15; Ethan Miller/Getty Images Sport/Getty Images, p.16; Kevin C. Cox/Getty Images Sport/Getty Images, p.17; Paras Griffin/Getty Images Sport/Getty Images, p.18; Christian Petersen/Getty Images Sport/Getty Images, p.19; Rich von Biberstein/Icon Sportswire/Getty Images, p.20; Mitchell Leff/Getty Images Sport/Getty Images, p.21; Mitchell Leff/Getty Images Sport/Getty Images, p.22; Rich von Biberstein/Icon Sportswire/Getty Images, p.23; Abbie Parr/Getty Images Sport/Getty Images, p.24; Alex Slitz/Getty Images Sport/Getty Images, p.25; Ethan Miller/Getty Images Sport/Getty Images, p.26; Rich von Biberstein/Icon Sportswire/Getty Images, p.27; Erica Denhoff/Icon Sportswire/Getty Images, p.28; Paras Griffin/Getty Images Sport/Getty Images, p. 29

Cover image: Ethan Miller/Getty Images Sport/Getty Images